Wait For GOD to Speak

VALERIE STIRTMIRE

Wait For GOD to Speak

31-Day Devotional

iUniverse

WAIT FOR GOD TO SPEAK
31-DAY DEVOTIONAL

Copyright © 2021 Valerie Stirtmire.

All rights reserved. No part of this book may be used or reproduced by any means, graphic, electronic, or mechanical, including photocopying, recording, taping or by any information storage retrieval system without the written permission of the author except in the case of brief quotations embodied in critical articles and reviews.

Copyright © 2015 by The Lockman Foundation, La Habra, CA 90631. All rights reserved. For Permission To Quote information visit http://www.lockman.org/

Scripture quotations marked TPT are from The Passion Translation®. Copyright © 2017, 2018 by Passion & Fire Ministries, Inc. Used by permission. All rights reserved. ThePassionTranslation.com.

Scripture quotations marked NLT are taken from the Holy Bible, New Living Translation, copyright © 1996, 2004, 2015 by Tyndale House Foundation. Used by permission of Tyndale House Publishers, Inc., Carol Stream, Illinois 60188. All rights reserved.

iUniverse books may be ordered through booksellers or by contacting:

iUniverse
1663 Liberty Drive
Bloomington, IN 47403
www.iuniverse.com
844-349-9409

Because of the dynamic nature of the Internet, any web addresses or links contained in this book may have changed since publication and may no longer be valid. The views expressed in this work are solely those of the author and do not necessarily reflect the views of the publisher, and the publisher hereby disclaims any responsibility for them.

Any people depicted in stock imagery provided by Getty Images are models, and such images are being used for illustrative purposes only.
Certain stock imagery © Getty Images.

ISBN: 978-1-6632-1606-9 (sc)
ISBN: 978-1-6632-1607-6 (e)

Library of Congress Control Number: 2021901707

Print information available on the last page.

iUniverse rev. date: 01/27/2021

Dedication

This devotional is dedicated to those that will be helped through my "Pandemic Journey". First, my husband, my personal comedian and my best friend, Frederick. You have made me laugh when a lot of times I wanted to cry. You support me when even I think sometimes, I should just quit. Thank you for being that rock that keeps me grounded. I absolutely love you and have loved you for 36 years since the day we first met.

To my adult children, Anthony, Christian, Kameron, Mikayla and Kamelyn, you all keep me on my knees because I want nothing less than the best for you. You all are amazing adults and I love you dearly. To my granddaughter Alyssa, you are another reason I want to make a difference in every way I can. I want you to grow up knowing that G-ma loves God and loves you.

To my spiritual parents, Pastors Doug and Shay Taylor, thank you for seeing what I could not see in myself and pushing me to chase after all that God has for me. I love you two so much.

To my siblings, nieces, nephews and extended family. Thank you for your support as I follow the path God is leading me.

To my besties, Erica, Kim, Joyce, Evon, Darlene and Kim, you ladies rock and you have always supported me. Thank you for your love and your prayers. I love you all infinitely.

To everyone reading this book, thank you for taking this journey with me. The pandemic of 2020 birthed out what I have been hash tagging #waitforGodtospeakinprayer #intercessorriseup. This devotional is a compilation of the things the spirit of God spoke to me through my intimate time with Him. I pray that this devotional blesses you as it has blessed me.

Introduction

I must admit I had no idea that a book would come from my intimate time with God. This journey began with me wanting to hear from God in a more intimate way. The pandemic of 2020 had me stressed and nervous. We were on lockdown and not able to go to church. I missed the fellowship of my church family and I needed to hear from God in a major way to get back on track.

I started my mornings by going into my home office and reading anything I could get my hands on to get something to ignite me. I had 5 or 6 books I started reading looking for that one thing to jumpstart me. Finally, I just pulled out a devotional that a friend of mine had sent me and began to read it. It sparked something in me. I began to read and pray with more passion than I had in months. After that it was easier to get back on track and I began to read the Word of God and it was like the words came to life for me.

I started having worship time, I would listen to soft music, write down a scripture, pray and wait for God to speak. This has become my new normal. Sometimes I get the "Wow" moments and sometimes I get the ok it is time to do some studying. Either way I believe God is speaking. I go into everyday believing that God will speak to me.

The day I realized a simple interactive devotional would come from this was when I was talking to someone and I said the words from my mouth. I had not planned on saying that. I just went with it. Maybe that meant years down the line I would write a devotional. On December 19th, 2020 I awoke from a dream and I heard "write a 31-day devotional". I jumped up, went into my office, turned on my computer and then the doubts came. What in the world was I thinking? Write what? Where would I start?

I turned my worship music on waited on God to speak. What I had forgotten is that I had started recording voice memos of my morning meditation times with God. I picked my phone up to open the voice memo app and when I opened it, the last entry read "New Recording 31". I heard in my spirit it has already been written, you just need to put it on paper. Tears began to flow as I received confirmation that what I had heard was what God wanted me to do.

I began to listen to my entries and what I had written in my journal and it all began to come together. What I wanted to give to others was an opportunity to hear God speak. I wanted this devotional to be simple and interactive. It begins with a topic, scripture, encouraging words, a prayer and an area to apply your notes on what God is speaking.

My prayer is that this devotional will bless you and cause a fire to be ignited in your hearts to chase after and listen for the voice of God. #waitforGodtospeakinprayer

Blessings,
Valerie Stirtmire

Day 1

UP UNTIL NOW

John 16:24

Until now you have not asked [the Father] for anything in my name; but now ask and keep on asking and you will receive, so that your joy may be full and complete (AMP)

You must believe that your slate has been wiped clean that up until now every little thing that you have done is null and void to God. You must determine in your heart today that God will accomplish much in and through you. Yesterday is nothing compared to what God is preparing for you today.

PRAYER

God, I thank you that my preparation time is over and that My time is now.

NOTES

Day 2

PROTECTING MY MOST VALUABLE POSSESSION

Job 33:4

The Spirit of God has made me, And the breath of the Almighty gives me life [which inspires me]. [AMP]

My spiritual life is my greatest and most valuable possession. The breath of God gives me life. He created me for this purpose. I will never again allow someone else to define me, from my up until now moment my slate has been washed clean.

PRAYER

God, show me how to protect my most valuable possession, this spiritual life you have given me so that I might stay connected and in tune with you.

NOTES

Day 3

MY ASSIGNMENT COMES FROM GOD

Isaiah 48:10

Indeed, I have refined you, but not as silver; I have tested and chosen you in the furnace of affliction. [AMP]

I cannot be jealous or intimidated by someone else's anointing. It is not the calling/anointing that gets me into trouble, it is my character or lack of character. How do I act when I want a "yes" but get a "no"? Draw a line in the sand today and choose what you are about. Is it your assignment that you have been tested and chosen for or is it the accolades of man which are fleeting? Choose assignment. Do not get jealous of others get motivated to do what God has assigned you to do.

PRAYER

God, help me to not focus on someone else's gift but to choose to be motivated about what you have given me to do.

NOTES

Day 4

GOD'S PART IN MY LIFE

Lamentations 3:24-25

"The Lord is my portion and my inheritance," says my soul; "Therefore I have hope in Him and wait expectantly for Him." The Lord is good to those who wait [confidently for Him, To those who seek Him [on the authority of God's word]. [AMP]

God is our portion because this is what our soul says. Therefore, I can hope in Him because He is good to those who wait on Him and whose soul seeks Him. Because my soul has connected to the fact that God is my part of the whole, He is the part that gives me whole life goodness. His part is the most valuable part.

PRAYER

God, I need you first for anything else to come to me or for anything in my life to come together.

NOTES

Day 5

TELL OTHERS

Mark 5:19

Jesus answered, "No." but said to him, Go back to your home and to your family and tell them what the Lord has done for you. Tell them how he had mercy on you." [TPT]

Exciting experiences will cause you to take what you have learned and give it to others. Tell others that this is your God-given ability by using the gifts, He has given you, well. You tell others by serving others. You tell others by living a life surrendered to Jesus.

PRAYER

God, help me to sit at your feet and get what I need for this journey so that I might tell others.

NOTES

Day 6

EXAMINE AND SEE GOOD

Psalms 34:8

O taste and see that the Lord [our God] is good; How blessed [fortunate, prosperous, and favored by God] is the man who takes refuge in Him. [AMP]

Sometimes we must stop and look at the small portion of a situation or circumstance and examine what is trying to get us off course or out of focus. Then we must forgo the bad we want to see in order to see the good God has for us. Put your trust in God and you will be able to examine and see good and not only will you see good, but you will see how good God truly is.

PRAYER

God, help me to see the good when my mind wants to only see the bad. Help me to stay focused on you.

NOTES

Day 7

CALL AND HE WILL ANSWER

Jeremiah 33:3

Call unto me, and I will answer thee, and shew the great and mighty things, which thou knowest not. [KJV]

God has the answers that we need, but in order to get those answers we must call upon His name. The great things that we want to see happening in our lives are a result of seeking God. Those things that we do not know about can be seen when we seek God's face.

PRAYER

God, I call out to you to give me not only the answers for my day but the answers for my future.

NOTES

Day 8

SWIFT TO HEAR, SLOW TO SPEAK

James 1:19

"Wherefore, my beloved brethren, let every man be swift to hear, slow to speak, slow to wrath:" [KJV]

Listening for real is a job and listening without speaking is overtime on that job. Sometimes just listening can be hard task especially if you do not agree, but we must listen in order to gain wisdom on how to deal with someone else's problems and pain.

PRAYER

God, help me to listen and be slow to judge when I speak so that I might be effective enough to help someone else.

NOTES

Day 9

PARTNERS TO YOUR VISION

Habakkuk 2:1-2

"I will stand upon my watch, and set me upon the tower, and will watch to see what he will say unto me, and what I shall answer when I am reproved. And the Lord answered me, and said, Write the vision, make it plain upon tables, that he may run that readeth it." [KJV]

Does anyone besides you know that your vision for your family, for your career, for every aspect of your life is? The word in Habakkuk 2:2 says write the vision and make it plain, sometimes we stop there, and we have written so many visions that even we do not know what the vision is anymore. The latter part of that scripture gives others a part in your vision, it says "so that those that read it may run with it". How can someone run with to share our vision if we have not made it plain, so they understand their part? Starting today I must be honest with God and myself and say I will write the vision so plain that the people assigned to run with it know their role and they are released to run.

PRAYER

God, help me share my vision with those assigned to help me so that I might accomplish your plan for my life.

NOTES

Day 10

COUNT THE COST

Luke 14:27-30

"And whosoever doth not bear his cross, and come after me, cannot be my disciple. For which of you, intending to build a tower, sitteth not down first, and counteth the cost, whether he have sufficient to finish it? Lest haply, after he hath laid the foundation, and is not able to finish it, all that behold it begin to mock him, Saying, This man began to build, and was not able to finish." [KJV]

You must count the cost. Sometimes you must sit down and think about what you are doing, then think about what you need to be doing. If the two are not leading you in the same direction, change course. Even if you have been boasting about is not the plan, REPENT and go in the direction God is leading you. Do not be so high-minded that you miss God. The Kingdom of God needs you to be and ASSET not a LIABILITY!

PRAYER

God, help me to sit down and count the cost in every decision I make.

NOTES

_____

_____

_____

_____

Day 11

YES, IS YES AND NO IS NO

Matthew 5:37

"But let your communication be, Yea, yea; Nay, nay: for whatsoever is more that these cometh of evil." [KJV]

Let your yes be yes and your no be no. Not everything needs explaining. Stop talking!! Not everything deserves your voice. Somethings deserve your silence while God works.

PRAYER

God, help me to make a decision and stick with it.

NOTES

Day 12

REINFORCEMENTS HAVE BEEN DISPATCHED

Romans 1:12

When we get together, I want to encourage you in your faith, but I also want to be encouraged by yours." [NLT]

Start declaring that your reinforcements have been dispatched and these reinforcements have power. They are ready and they are equipped. Help is not only on the way, but your help also has what you need.

PRAYER

God, grant my reinforcements the ability to help me and give me the ability to help them.

NOTES

Day 13

PROTECT OUR POSITION

Jeremiah 29:11

"For I know the thoughts that I think toward you, saith the Lord, thoughts of peace, and not of evil, to give you and expected end." [KJV]

As you listen and wait on God and seek to please Him, God will protect your position. What position you ask? Positions in Him, positions in your family, positions in your careers and positions in every aspect of your life. As God protects your position, He has also planned your future. Get your expectancy level up.

PRAYER

God, thank you for the plans that you have for my life and my future.

NOTES

Day 14

FORGIVE

Matthew 5:23-24

"Therefore if thou bring thy gift to the altar, and there rememberest that thy brother hath ought against thee; Leave there thy gift before the altar, and go thy way; first be reconciled to thy brother, and then come and offer thy gift." [KJV]

Not forgiving others and anger can produce hurt. These along with resentment can taint your heart and your spirit. This scripture comes alive by saying if you are in your prayer time offering your gift to God and you receive wisdom that you need to forgive someone, stop and forgive quickly then go back to God in prayer. Decide to forgive, do not debate forgiveness. Forgive and let it go. You have work to do. Do not be your own hindrance.

PRAYER

God, help me to forgive and let go so that I may move forward with my life and future.

NOTES

Day 15

CONFIDENCE TOWARD GOD

1 John 3:20-22

"For if our heart condemn us, God is greater than our heart, and knoweth all things. Beloved, if our heart condemn us not, then have we confidence toward God. And whatsoever we ask, we receive of him, because we keep his commandments, and do those things that are pleasing in his sight." [KJV]

There is a time to pray but there is also a time to deal with our sin. You know that thing that people do not know about, but God does. There is a time to deal with sin so that when you pray you are not preying. Do not give the enemy a door. Do not let your heart issues cause you to miss it. You must deal with the sin so that you can have that confidence that whatsoever you ask God for you will receive it.

PRAYER

God, help me to keep my heart in check so that I may have confidence that what I ask for in prayer I will receive.

NOTES

Day 16

YOU SHALL RECEIVE POWER

Acts 1:8

But you will receive power when the Holy Spirit comes upon you. And you will be my witnesses, telling people about me everywhere—in Jerusalem, throughout Judea, in Samaria, and to the ends of the earth. [NLT]

When you understand that you have power from above, you also realize that you can do amazing things. Take time today to ask God for power to do what he has planned for you to do. Once you receive the power the Holy Spirit comes upon you to lead and direct you on how to use that power. Use your power to help someone else and to let others know that there is hope for their future.

PRAYER

God, give me power and the Holy Spirit so that I might do the work you have for me to do.

NOTES

Day 17

DO NOT QUIT

Isaiah 50:7

"Because the Sovereign Lord helps me, I will not be disgraced. Therefore, I have set my face like a stone, determined to do his will. And I know that I will not be put to shame." [NLT]

Keep moving. Keep Going. Hold on and listen for God's voice. Change the narrative for your life by not quitting in your mind or heart. God has plans for you. Do not get discouraged and do not faint. Keep going because the benefits are there but only when you do not give up. It is perfectly ok to get tired, just do not quit!

PRAYER

Lord, help me to stay strong and not get discouraged even when circumstances say I should give up.

NOTES

Day 18

USE YOUR VOICE

Jeremiah 1:11-12

The word of the Lord came to me, saying Jeremiah, what do you see? And I said I see the branch of an almond tree. Then the Lord said to me You have seen well, for I am actively watching over my word to fulfill it. [AMP]

The sound of your voice should activate something. Jeremiah gave God dialogue that activated a response from God. Jeremiah said "I see a branch". God's response to that was that he had seen well. Use your voice to speak God's Word into your life. The scripture above says that God is actively watching over His Word to fulfill it. God is waiting on you to speak what is written, not what is convenient.

PRAYER

God, help me to speak your word no matter what situation I find myself in. I will use my voice to declare your word because you are actively listening so that you might fulfill it.

NOTES

Day 19

TIME TO REGROUP

Isaiah 1:18-19

Come now, let us reason together, saith the Lord: though your sins be as scarlet, they shall be as white as snow; though they be red like crimson, they shall be as wool. If ye be willing and obedient, ye shall eat the good of the land: [KJV]

Perhaps God is saying to you I already know who you are and what you are capable of but if you take the time and sit down with me and REGROUP, I can make you a promise. To reason with someone means you have to think through something logically and induce a change of opinion through presentation. So if God wants to reason with you He is willing to listen to your side of the story. After you have laid all the pain and pressure out before Him, allow God to recalibrate your life and make it better. Verse 19 above lets you know that if you are willing and obedient to the process you will receive good. So why not let take the time to regroup so your life might be better.

PRAYER

God, help me regroup, I have done it my way long enough, now I want to do it your way.

NOTES

_____

_____

_____

_____

Day 20

PRESERVED FOR PURPOSE

Proverbs 19:21

You can make many plans, but the Lord's purpose will prevail. [NLT]

You were carefully crafted and picked out by God. Do not allow mistakes of the past to creep in and make you believe you are less than what God designed you to be. We find our purpose in God by dropping or stripping ourselves of the excuses that would cause us to become an enemy to our own purpose. We find our purpose by separating our purposeful selves from our past selves. We are chosen. Do not waste another minute with the enemy downplaying yourself. Get up, dust yourself off and let God's purpose prevail in your life.

NOTES

Day 21

IT IS WORKING TOGETHER

Romans 8:28

And we know that all things work together for good to them that love God, to them who are the called according to his purpose. [KJV]

We must realize that all things work together, and when they work together, that they are not just working together but they are working together for GOOD. We also have a responsibility to work together with people. If things can work together so can people.

PRAYER

God, because things are working together for my good, please send the right people into my life that will work with me and not against me.

NOTES

Day 22

IT IS A HEART ISSUE

Psalms 51:10

Create in me a clean heart, O God. Renew a loyal spirit within me. [NLT]

Sometimes it is not others, but it is us and our heart issues. If we are easily offended that will take a toll on our hearts. We begin to see someone in a different light when what we should be doing is checking the condition of our own heart daily. We must ask God to show us who we are so that we might be sure that we are not rebelling. Ask God to create a clean heart and to renew a loyal spirit in you daily.

PRAYER

God, here is my heart, mold it into what you desire not what I desire because I get lost in my feelings sometimes. Help me to receive a clean heart and loyal spirit.

NOTES

Day 23

FILTER OUT THE FOOLISHNESS OF THIS WORLD

1 Corinthians 2:14

But the natural man receiveth not the things of the Spirit of God: for they are foolishness unto him: neither can he know them, because they are spiritually discerned.

Naturally, the things that we do for God do not make sense to people who do not believe in God. It is our job to make sure that we are presenting what we receive in a way that anyone could understand. We must seek the wisdom of God so that we might give the wisdom of God, not what we think or feel. The goal is to win those who are trying to do life on their own.

PRAYER

God, help me to get me out of the way when sharing the love and wisdom of God with others.

NOTES

Day 24

LIFT JESUS UP

John 12:32

And I, if I be lifted up from the earth, will draw all men unto me. [KJV]

Allow this scripture to come alive in you, so that you might get the true understanding of what Jesus is saying. Jesus was speaking of the way He would die but also, He was giving us as the believer hope for our future. Yes, the cross was lifted up once He was nailed to it, but even in this sacrifice Jesus was in a position where He had to be looked up to. Today let us still look up to Jesus so that people might be drawn unto Him as our Savior.

PRAYER

God, help me to lift Jesus up so that people who encounter me would be drawn to Jesus.

NOTES

Day 25

REACH THOSE ASSIGNED TO YOU

John 17:12

While I was with them in the world, I kept them in thy name: those that thou gavest me I have kept, and none of them is lost, but the son of perdition; that the scripture might be fulfilled. [KJV]

Draw a line in the sand today and choose what you are about. Is it assignment or the likes of man? Do not worry about the likes or dislikes of man. Reach the ones you are supposed to reach. Make an impact and inspire those that God has assigned to you.

PRAYER

God, please show me who I am assigned to so that I might make an impact in and inspire them to be great. It is not always about me, but the ones I must reach for You.

NOTES

Day 26

GOD IS MY PORTION

Lamentations 3:24-25

The LORD is my portion, saith my soul; therefore will I hope in him. The LORD is good unto them that wait for him, to the soul that seeketh him. [KJV]

God is my portion because my soul says so. That is why I can have hope in Him. God is good to those who wait on Him and the person whose soul seeks Him. Because my soul has already connected to the fact that God is my part of the whole, He is the part that gives me whole life goodness. God's part is the most valuable part of me.

PRAYER

God, I need you first for anything else to work for me or for anything to come together for me.

NOTES

Day 27

WATCH

Luke 12:37

Blessed are those servants who the lord when he cometh shall find watching: verily I say unto you that he shall gird himself, and make them to sit down to meat, and will come forth and serve them. [KJV]

Discernment (the ability to decide between truth and error or right and wrong) comes through watching. Let God find you watching. Let the enemy find you on your post watching. Let those who trust you find you watching. Take the time to understand the things that are happening around you.

PRAYER

God, help me to be mindful of the things that are going on around me and to watch and stay focused.

NOTES

Day 28

DO NOT BE MOVED

Psalm 16:8

I have set the LORD always before me: because he is at my right hand, I shall not be moved. [KJV]

The old nature of us is determined to get our attention and keep us focused on what we used to be or what we used to do. During these times is when we must focus on God because He is close to me and available. My confidence will never be shaken because I experience God's wrap-around presence every moment.

PRAYER

God, thank you that I experience your presence every moment and every day to keep me from being moved by the things that happen around me.

NOTES

Day 29

TEACH OTHERS

2 Timothy 2:2

And the things that thou hast heard of me among many witnesses, the same commit thou to faithful men, who shall be able to teach others also. [KJV]

The things that you have learned, teach others. Too often we want to train others to do what we say rather than what we do. We want to pick people who will not buck the system we created. That is called cloning not calling. When we train those God has assigned us to, we get to pass on what God has called us to do. Develop, cultivate and grow people to honor God with their life.

PRAYER

God, help me to train others to be who you want them to be not a carbon copy of who I am.

NOTES

Day 30

CARE ABOUT WHAT MATTERS TO JESUS

Philippians 2:21

All the others care only for themselves and not for what matters to Jesus Christ. [NLT]

Let us be careful in a time where everyone is busy seeking what is best for themselves that we do not get caught up in these ways. We should instead seek after the things that are most important to our Lord and Savior, Jesus Christ. If we find ourselves in a place of self-fulfillment and not wanting to help anyone along the way we must repent, turn from that mind set and ask God to help us change.

PRAYER

God, help me to not be self-absorbed and self-focused but to be aware that what matters to Jesus should matter to me.

NOTES

Day 31

YOU HAVE BEEN SENT

John 20:21-23

Then said Jesus to them again, Peace be unto you: as my Father hath sent me, even so send I you. And when he had said this, he breathed on them, and saith unto them, Receive ye the Holy Ghost: Whose soever sins ye remit, they are remitted unto them; and whose soever sins ye retain, they are retained. [KJV]

Jesus said just as my Father has sent me, I send you. Receive the Holy Spirit as a comforter and guide. Go teach forgiveness of sins and sins will be forgiven. If we refuse to tell of this forgiveness people will remain bound to the sin. Teach the people what you have been sent to teach.

PRAYER

God, help me to teach others what I have learned so that they may likewise teach someone else.

NOTES

Bonus

MY MOST INTIMATE PRAYERS

Some of my most intimate prayers to God have not been long and drawn out but simple and heartfelt and based from the scriptures. I have chosen to share some of those with you, in hopes that they will bless you as they have me.

God, I thank you for expunging my sin as I put my trust in Jesus today. I thank you that your sustaining grace is sufficient enough for me. I thank you greater are You that resides within me than he that is in the world. 1 John 4:4 [KJV]

God, when I ask You what is in this lifestyle that I have chosen to live for You, I thank you that Your answer to me is that You give me a future in You. Jeremiah 29:11 [NLT]

God, I thank you for my time of necessary pruning, as I look at my life and see what may be keeping me from producing more. Once I recognize what that may be, it is my job to cut it off. I know the longer I take to cut it off, the stronger the danger is of me growing weak and losing my relationship with You. John 15:2-6 [KJV]

God, I thank you that You release favor for me to always have enough. Proverbs 3:4 [KJV]

God, help me identify the false that would show up in my life to try to corrupt me. Matthew 7:15-17 [KJV]

God, I thank you for exposing me to more so that You might expand my capacity to love Your people and to teach Your people. This world is in a spiritual crisis. Evil has permeated the hearts of people. Help them live. Help them come into the light. Help them love. John 3:19 [KJV]

God, sometimes I go overboard with my independence and act as if I do not need You. Help me to understand that situations in my life will not fix themselves. I must realize that if my heart does not condemn me when I get off track that I can still come to You and ask with confidence what I need from You when it is in Your will. 1 John 3:20-22

Made in the USA
Coppell, TX
11 December 2022